ARABINESQUE-AT-LAW

Arabinesque-at-law

Duncan. What bloody man is that ?
Malcolm. This is the serjeant.

Macbeth, act I, sc. i.

Hon. Sir Robert Megarry

London
Wildy & Sons Ltd
1969

The net profits of this edition go to the
Barristers' Benevolent Association

First published in 1969
by Wildy & Sons Ltd, Lincoln's Inn Archway,
Lincoln's Inn, London W.C.2

Printed in Great Britain by
W. & J. Mackay & Co. Ltd, Chatham, Kent, England

To

RAYNER GODDARD

sometime Lord Chief Justice of England

without permission

but

with warm affection

Prolegomena

IN 1843 THERE appeared a little book of sixteen small pages entitled *Arabiniana*, with a prefatory note initialled H.B.C. as the only indication of authorship. The book recorded some of the more remarkable dicta of Serjeant Arabin, uttered in his judicial capacity at the Old Bailey in the fourth decade of the nineteenth century. In 1911 Sir Frederick Pollock gave the book some publicity in an article in the *Cornhill Magazine* which was reprinted (with corrections) in 1922 in his *Essays in the Law*.[1] But that was half a century ago, and he reproduced part or all of only about a quarter of the cases in the book. Very few copies of the book seem to exist,[2] and it has long dropped out of sight. Yet it is too good[3]—and too bad—for that.

I have accordingly ventured to revive the book. The simplest course would have been to reprint it as it stood; but there seemed to be some advantage in trying to produce a less segmented and more cursive text than that of the original, giving greater prominence to the Arabinaics. I had my

[1] See pp. 287–300.
[2] Pollock tells us that it was reprinted in Philadelphia in 1846, but that the edition was of only twelve copies, and he had been unable to trace any of them: *op. cit.*, p. 298.
[3] Sydney Smith described the book to Lord Murray as 'very witty and humorous': *op. cit.*, p. 299. Lush J. perhaps cited it in *Leverson* v. *The Queen* (1869) 10 B. & S. 404 at 412.

copy with me on what proved to be a long, rainy Long Vacation week-end at Geiranger, hard by the encouraging diapason of an engorged Norwegian waterfall; and this book is the result. In it I have removed to the footnotes much of the encumbering material such as the names of the cases, the dates, the reporters' initials, and the like; and I have freely revised the sequence of cases and the introductory texts. Where the original states the verdict I have, of course, included it; but in giving the dates of the cases it has usually seemed unnecessary to reproduce more than the year.

I have omitted H.B.C.'s cross-headings. Some were neat and apt, but many were disappointing, and in any case they impeded the flow of the text. *Of beer* could not do justice to *R.* v. *Higgins*; nor was *R.* v. *Chilston and Chandler* adequately proclaimed by *Of principles, axioms and the like*. Throughout, *res ipsa loquitur*. *Per contra*, I would not wish and have not dared to alter or omit a single word or comma of the Serjeant's; apart from the suppression of some italics, everything of his is reproduced exactly as it appeared in *Arabiniana*, complete and unabridged, as they say. I have, however, corrected a patent slip in the report of *R.* v. *George Tolly*, and added seven extra cases from other sources. I suspect that a careful examination of other literature would reveal further reports;[4] but the fjords offered few facilities for legal research, and since my return my natural indolence has reasserted itself. I have also provided a table of cases and an index;

[4] We have Pollock's assurance that the dictum 'Prisoner, God has given you good abilities, instead of which you go about the country stealing ducks' was uttered not by Arabin but by Rev. Mr Alderson (a cousin of Alderson B.) when sitting as chairman of Sheffield Quarter Sessions: *op. cit.*, pp. 297, 298.

had the rain stopped sooner the index would have been shorter.

Perhaps some further and better particulars should be added. Of the eighty-four cases in *Arabiniana*, sixty-nine are reported by H.B.C.; and he states that he is 'responsible for the strict verbal accuracy' of these. The other fifteen are vouched by nine other sets of initials. C.P. leads with five reports, J.'E. and F.P.W. come next with two each, and W.B., M.C., R.N.C., R.D., J.H. *et al.* and D.D.K. provide one each. Pollock thought it right to refrain from identifying H.B.C. and his fellow reporters,[5] and in this I bow to his judgment. They were all, I think, practising barristers, so that the destination of any profit from this edition of their work seems appropriate.

The earliest case reported was *R.* v. *Gough and Others* on December 30, 1830, and the latest case was *R.* v. *Harewood* on August 13, 1839, so that the reports span nearly nine years; but most of them date from 1832 and 1833. As in *Arabiniana*, 'A.P.' and 'P.P.' (which are not invariably given) respectively signify *Ante Prandium* and *Post Prandium*; but like Sir Frederick Pollock I have failed to detect any difference in quality attributable either to food or to any concomitant of it. The inspired misquotation on the title page is reproduced as it appears in *Arabiniana*; the original in Act I, Scene ii of *Macbeth* runs—

DUNCAN. What bloody man is that? He can report,
   As seemeth by his plight, of the revolt
   The newest state.
MALCOLM.   This is the sergeant.

[5] See *op. cit.*, p. 290; but *cp.* p. 294.

The bare facts of Arabin's career may be stated shortly.[6] William St Julien Arabin seems to have been born in about 1775, the son of General Arabin, on whose death he succeeded to extensive estates in Middlesex and Essex. He was educated at St Paul's School and Corpus Christi College, Cambridge, and after being called to the Bar by the Inner Temple on May 8, 1801, he practised on the Home Circuit and at the Old Bailey and other metropolitan sessions. On October 11, 1803, he married the eldest daughter of Richard Meux. By 1823 he had become one of the judges of the Courts of the Sheriffs of London and Middlesex; and on May 13, 1824, he and Thomas Wilde (later to become Lord Truro L.C.) were 'called to the degree of the coif, and gave rings, with the following motto: "Regi regnoque fidelis"'.[7]

At about the same time Arabin became Deputy Judge Advocate of the Army, an office which he retained until his death, apart from a period from November 24, 1838, until February, 1839, when he held the higher post of Judge Advocate-General of the Army. But the offices by which he will be remembered were those of the 'third civic judge' (i.e. the judge next after the Recorder and the Common Ser-

---

[6] See Pollock, *op. cit.*, p. 288; *Annual Register, 1841, Appendix to Chronicle*, pp. 239, 240, described by Pollock as 'a short and not too careful obituary notice' (p. 288); *The Times*, December 17, 1841, p. 4 (to which the account in the *Annual Register* is closely similar); the *Gentleman's Magazine* vol. 73, p. 987, vol. 17 (N.S.) 219; (1930) 170 *Notes & Queries* 309 (and see p. 310, suggesting that Arabin was the original of Serjeant Snubbin in *Pickwick Papers*); J. A. Venn, *Alumni Cantabrigienses*, Part II, vol. 1 (1940), p. 65; various volumes of *The Law List*; and 2 Bing. 1.

[7] 2 Bing. 1.

jeant) at the Old Bailey, to which he was elected in 1827[8] when the New Court was built, and one of the Commissioners at the Central Criminal Court when it was constituted by the Central Criminal Court Act, 1834. He continued in this office until his death at his residence, High Beech, Essex, on December 15, 1841, *aet.* 66. He was, it was said, 'very much attached to agricultural pursuits, in which he was extensively engaged, and enjoyed the reputation of exercising benevolence among the poor living on his respective estates'.[9]

Pollock approved the description of Arabin as 'an original, absent, eccentric man, not wanting in mother wit, but very much so in the faculty of expressing himself rationally'.[10] Serjeant Ballantine described him as 'a shrewd, quaint little man', who 'enunciated absurdities with most perfect innocence'.[11] Another of his contemporaries, Serjeant Robinson, said that he was 'a thin, old, wizen-faced man, very eccentric in his ideas and expressions, and more so in his logic'.[12] He was 'very short-sighted, and also very deaf';[13] and the notes that he made 'were almost undecipherable by anybody, himself included. The letters were unformed enough, but his figures were much worse.'[14]

He does indeed seem to have been a true original. The passage of more than a century has done something to soften

[8] But see (1923) 39 L.Q.R. 132, suggesting that he was appointed in 1824 or 1825.
[9] *The Times*, December 17, 1841, p. 4.
[10] *Op. cit.*, p. 287.
[11] *Serjeant Ballantine's Experiences* (8th ed. 1883) p. 55.
[12] Mr Serjeant Robinson, *Bench and Bar* (2nd ed. 1889) p. 43.
[13] *Ibid.*, p. 44.
[14] *Ibid.*, p. 252.

the sense of outrage which cases such as *R.* v. *Anon.* (1831) bring to us today; but by no means all of his eccentricities favoured the prosecution, and many were harmless enough. The extracts reported below are minute in relation to all the words which he must have uttered during his fourteen years on the criminal bench; yet even so, in his court the dominant atmosphere must at times have been a simple wonderment at what he would say next. No literary monument to British justice should ever ignore Arabin. He achieved a galimatias[15] of language and thought that had on the bench neither pride of ancestry nor, one prays, hope of posterity. Yet he was; and in his uniquity he deserves preservation. *Requiescat.*

Lincoln's Inn.
All Saints' Day, 1968.   R. E. M.

---

[15] See *Andrew* v. *Murdoch* (1814) 2 Dow 401 at 431, *per* Lord Holland.

Table of Cases

Table of Abbreviations

A.P.   Ante prandium
Arab. H.B.C., *Arabiniana* (1843)
P.P.   Post prandium

Rob.   Mr Serjeant Robinson (B. C.
Robinson), *Bench and Bar*
(2nd ed., 1889)

PLAINLY THE COURT had physical limitations. Counsel once complained of excessive ventilation.

> *The Court :* Yes. When I sit here, I fancy myself on the top of Mount Breeze; and the first thing I do every morning of the session, is to go to the glass and see if my eyes have not been blown out of my head.[1]

There were noises, too.

> *The Court :* I must turn the Court out. Mr Wontner, do commit somebody. I must have silence. It is quite indecent. The courts of justice are open, and I must put an end to it.[2]

Again,

> *The Court :* Silence. The Court is not to be borne. We must not keep going on as we used to do here.[3]

Personally, however, the Court was without blemish. It had instant percipience.

> *The Court*, to witness: Now, mind: we sit here day after day, year after year, hour after hour, and can see through a case in a moment.[4]

Again, on an indictment for stealing a handkerchief, one of the two prisoners, one Buckley, asked a witness whether he saw him with the handkerchief, to which the witness replied 'No'. The prisoner was convicted, and then—

---

[1] *Anon.* (1838) Arab. 11, *ex rel.* C.P.
[2] *R.* v. *Deadman and Petty* (1832) Arab. 11, P.P.
[3] *R.* v. *Inscape* (1834) Arab. 11, A.P., *ex rel.* C.P.
[4] *R.* v. *Ford* (1831) Arab. 4, P.P.

The Court, to Buckley: The moment I heard your question, I knew that you were both practised thieves—common pickpockets.[5]

The Court also had a good memory for prisoners' faces, whatever their youth and origin.

The Court : This is not the first time I have seen your face, young gentleman, and that you have seen mine. You know very well we have met before.

Prisoner : No, it's the first time I was ever here, your worship. I hope you'll have mercy, my lord.

The Court : Don't tell me that. I can't be deceived. Your face is very familiar to me. Gaoler, do you know anything of this youngster?

Gaoler : Oh! yes, my lord; he's a very bad boy, a constant associate of thieves. He's been very badly brought up, my lord. His mother keeps a disreputable house in Whitechapel.

The Court : Ah, I knew I was right. I was quite sure your face was well known to me.[6]

But such assertions were merely part of the Court's proclaimed omnicompetent infallibility:

'I know what's what';[7]

'I never forget anything';[8]

'I am not a fool';[9] and

'We have not lived here all our lives for nothing'.[10]

[5] *R.* v. *Buckley and Robinson* (1832) Arab. 4, P.P.

[6] *Anon.* (n.d.) Rob. 48.

[7] *R.* v. *Brown* (1833) Arab. 4, P.P.

[8] *R.* v. *Kilburn* (1832) Arab. 3, P.P.

[9] *R.* v. *Williams* (1833) Arab. 3, A.P.

[10] *R.* v. *Taylor* (1832) Arab. 4.

Such a Court plainly could not fall into the error of compounding a felony. Thus on an indictment for stealing thirty-five shillings from the person, the case was proved; the prisoners then put in a receipt for thirty shillings signed by the prosecutor over a twopenny stamp, in part payment of the money stolen, and in full of all demands.

> *The Court*, in charge. The lower orders—I mean, the lower class of persons, never seem to understand, that in all courts of criminal justice the King is the person who carries on the prosecution, and is supposed to lose the money. I cannot, if so disposed, compound a felony—the King alone can.[11]

The Court's special skills included those of conducting exceptionally speedy trials, and of accurately predicting the duration of any case.

> *The Court*, to Jonas, Clerk of the Arraigns: Now, Mr Jonas, why did you put off this case? I can try it in five minutes; and it will take any other judge, whoever he may be, two hours.[12]

But when a case in which there were three witnesses was called on at 3 p.m.—

> *The Court*: Gentlemen, this will be a long case. My judicial eye never deceives me: I see that it will not be over by one o'clock to-morrow morning, and I want to be away at four. The case must stand over.[13]

The Court's eyesight was remarkable, too. One witness who had identified a prisoner admitted in cross-examination that he had never been closer to him than eighty yards.

[11] *R.* v. *Smith, North and Bullock* (1832) Arab. 12, P.P.
[12] *R.* v. *Coppin* (1833) Arab. 3, P.P., *ex rel.* F.P.W.
[13] *R.* v. *Lewis* (1832) Arab. 4, A.P., *ex rel.* C.P.

> *Churchill*, for prisoner: Did you not say that you were
> induced to watch him because you did not like the
> look of his eye?
>
> *Witness:* Yes.
>
> *Churchill:* What! see a man's eye at eighty yards?
>
> *The Court:* Yes, to be sure. So can I; and guess pretty
> well what he is about, too.[14]

The Court's knowledge embraced all districts, and the
future as well as the past. On an indictment for stealing a
fowl—

> *The Court*, in charge: I know, of my own knowledge,
> that there is not a little hen-roost near town that is not
> robbed continually.[15]

And on an indictment for stealing a truss of hay—

> *Prosecutor:* In nine months I've been robbed seven
> times.
>
> *The Court:* I know it. There's scarcely anybody that
> lives in the country that is not robbed every day in the
> year.[16]

When a little boy was called up for judgment—

> *The Court:* Prisoner at the bar, when I saw you first I
> knew you as well as possible; when you began to cry
> I knew you still better. You have been here four times;
> I'm tired of the sight of you. You must go out of the
> country.[17]

Again, when a prisoner urged in his defence that he had
never been at the Old Bailey before—

[14] *R.* v. *John Lea* (1831) Arab. 4, A.P.
[15] *R.* v. *Wincks* (1832) Arab. 4, A.P.
[16] *R.* v. *Joseph Powell* (1832) Arab. 4, *ex rel.* R.D.
[17] *R.* v. *Anon.* (1831) Arab. 3, A.P. *ex rel.* C.P.

4

The Court: 'Tis of no use denying it, I recollect you perfectly well.

The prisoner: I meant, that I have never been transported before.

The Court, with a benignant smile: Then you shall be now.[18]

And—

The Court, to witness: Did you ever buy a horse of the prisoner?

Witness: No.

The Court: Then you did not pay him a five-pound note for that horse?

Payne, for prisoner: I am about to submit—

The Court: I cannot hear you. I know what you are about to say; and it is so monstrous and preposterous—[19]

The Court also commanded general recognition as a prophet of doom narrowly averted.

The Court, in charge: If this man had not been detected, any servant in the house might have been suspected, and every member of the family must have been irretrievably ruined. The worthy magistrate on the bench agrees with me, but that you might have known without my telling you.[20]

Was there, perhaps, some twinkle in counsel's eye when the following colloquy occurred? There had been a conference

---

[18] *R.* v. *Anon.* (1826) 39 L.Q.R. 132, citing *The Mirror*, January 7, 1826.

[19] *R.* v. *Parish Dighton* (1835) Arab. 5, A.P.

[20] *R.* v. *Brown* (1833) Arab. 14, P.P.

between the *Court*, *Phillips*, and *Clarkson*; and the prisoner
then pleaded Guilty.

> *The Court:* Mr Phillips, you must distinctly under-
> stand that I know nothing of this arrangement.
>
> *Phillips:* Yes, my lord; it is thoroughly understood
> that your lordship knows nothing.
>
> *The Court:* Certainly.[1]

There are glimpses of the Court fulfilling its accustomed
role of counsel for the undefended.[2] Thus—

> *The Court:* Mr Barry, do you prosecute?
>
> *Barry:* No, my lord.
>
> *The Court:* Then, I do. Here goes.[3]

And when the prosecutor produced a certificate of a former
conviction—

> *The Court:* Did you get that from the clerk of the
> peace?
>
> *Witness:* No: a policeman gave it me.
>
> *The Court:* Oh, very well. Let it be read.[4]

And—

> *The Court,* in charge: The business of this great
> metropolis must be carried on, and tradesmen must
> be protected in the exercise of their functions; so it
> will be for you to say whether the prisoner is guilty.[5]

Again—

---

[1] *R.* v. *Harris* (1834) Arab. 5, A.P., *ex rel.* W.B.
[2] There is no explicit statement to this effect; but the four ensuing
cases are all grouped under the heading 'Of the judge as counsel for
the prisoner', which would be inept if the prisoner had been
defended.
[3] *R.* v. *Oakley* (1832) Arab. 10, A.P.
[4] *R.* v. *Harewood* (1839) Arab. 10, P.P.
[5] *R.* v. *John Kemp* (1833) Arab. 10, P.P.

The Court, in charge: Can you suppose that this is a fabricated story founded on falsehood, with no foundation in truth, because she swears—that is, that her credit is not good, because she marked these sovereigns to entrap—that is, you see, the property is found upon her, and she has it ?[6]

The Court did not bow readily to authority, even its own. When counsel said 'My lord, I have some cases to cite', the answer was brief and pointed:

The Court : I don't care anything for any cases whatever.[7]

The year 1831 yielded two answers to the question whether it was necessary to state the prosecutor's name correctly in an indictment. On September 14, an indictment charged the prisoner with stealing a silk dress, the goods of Samuel Biss; the name proved was Samuel Benjamin Biss.

The Court : Then it is another person. Gentlemen, you must acquit the prisoner.[8]

On December 7, an indictment charged the prisoner with stealing a pair of shoes, the goods of James Rowe; the name proved was James Arundel Rowe, and counsel for the prisoner took the objection of misnomer.

The Court : There is nothing in the objection.[9]

Alibis, upheld even for the guilty in 1835, had fallen out of favour in 1839. In 1835—

The Court, in charge: The learned counsel is right in his position, and if he can show precisely at what

[6] *R.* v. *Theodosia Brown* (1833) Arab. 10, A.P.
[7] *R.* v. *Deadman and Petty* (1832) Arab. 11, P.P.; see also *R.* v. *Allen, post*, p. 13.
[8] *R.* v. *Holman* (1831) Arab. 3, P.P. Verdict, Not Guilty.
[9] *R.* v. *Watts* (1831) Arab. 3, A.P. Verdict, Guilty.

7

moment it was done, and that the prisoner was not there when he did it, and if so he could not do it. We cannot divest ourselves of common sense in courts of justice.[10]

But four years later, on an indictment for an offence sworn to at half past six o'clock on the Sunday before Easter, several witnesses testified in support of an alibi that the prisoner was in another place at that time.

The Court, in charge: A good deal has been said about the time, but we all know that in law sometimes the day is immaterial.[11]

The Court was forthright in its definitions. When a witness swore that the prosecutrix had said that the prisoner had stopped her and robbed her, counsel for the prisoner asked 'Did she not say, that the prisoner had *interrupted* her?'

The Court: That makes no difference; interrupting and robbing are the same thing.[12]

When another prisoner stood convicted—

The Court, to prisoner: I have no doubt of your guilt; you go into a public-house and break bulk, and drink beer; and that's what in law is called embezzlement.[13]

Again—

The Court, to witness: Was Rush off the premises?

Witness: Yes.

The Court: How long?

Witness: About four minutes.

The Court: Oh! then that's on the premises.[14]

[10] *R.* v. *Parish Dighton* (1835) Arab. 16, A.P.
[11] *R.* v. *Anon.* (1839) Arab. 16, A.P., *ex rel.* M.C.
[12] *R.* v. *Anon.* (1838) Arab. 16, A.P., *ex rel.* J.'E.
[13] *R.* v. *Higgins* (1839) Arab. 16, P.P., *ex rel.* J.'E.
[14] *R.* v. *Rush et al.* (1832) Arab. 9, P.P.

The interpretation of statutes was as vigorous. On an indictment for uttering counterfeit coin—

> *The Court*, to jury: Gentlemen, the lowest punishment is imprisonment for one year.
>
> *Ellis*, for prosecution: The words of the Act are, 'not exceeding one year'.
>
> *The Court:* Yes. But every good man would wish— Gentlemen, consider your verdict.[15]

And on an indictment for having bad money in possession, the Court explained how Parliament came to make a crime evidence of guilt.

> *The Court:* The legislature, finding that these utterances were carried on by persons on the other side of the street, enacted clauses making the felonious possession of bad money evidence of guilt.[16]

The Court had its own technique for examining witnesses. Thus—

> *The Court*, to witness: Were you in Tooley Street on the evening of the 24th?
>
> *Witness:* No, my lord.
>
> *The Court:* Did anything there attract your attention?
>
> *Witness:* No, my lord.
>
> *The Court:* What did you do upon that?[17]

Much was expected of them.

> *The Court:* My good man, don't go gabbling on so. Hold your tongue, and answer the question that is put to you.[18]

---

[15] *R.* v. *Walker* (1833) Arab. 13, P.P.
[16] *R.* v. *Sarah Peters* (1835) Arab. 16, P.P.
[17] *R.* v. *Dakes* (1833) Arab. 13, *cito* P.P.
[18] *Anon.* (n.d.) Rob. 48.

Again, on an indictment for stealing a pail of milk, one Jane Watson was examined by the Court.

> *The Court :* What is your husband's name ?
>
> *Witness :* I am not married.
>
> *The Court :* I mean he who is Ruth Watson.[19]

When Thomas Watson was examined by the Court—

> *The Court :* Is that your pail ?
>
> *Witness :* Yes.
>
> *The Court :* Well, although you are married, I suppose you are man enough to swear to a pail of milk.[20]

The verdict was Guilty.

> *The Court*, to prisoner: There! you are well out of this scrape.[1]

Where no counsel appeared, the Court itself examined the witness from the depositions; and it was not easily diverted from what it heard or did not hear. Once when the charge was stealing a pocket handkerchief, the Court happened instead to pick up the depositions in another case, in which a watch had been stolen.

> *The Court :* Well, witness, your name is John Tomkins.
>
> *Witness :* My lord, my name is Job Taylor.
>
> *The Court :* Ah! I see you are a sailor, and you live in the New Cut.
>
> *Witness :* No, my lord, I live at Wapping.
>
> *The Court :* Never mind your being out shopping. Had you your watch in your pocket on the 10th of November?
>
> *Witness :* I never had but one ticker, my lord, and that has been at the pawn-shop for the last six months.

[19] *R.* v. *Jarvis* (1832) Arab.12, P.P.
[20] *Ibid.*
[1] *Ibid.*

The Court: Who asked you how long you had had the watch? Why can't you say yes or no? Well, did you see the prisoner at the Bar?

Witness (a little confused): Yes, of course I did.

The Court: That's right, my man, speak up and answer shortly. Did the prisoner take your watch?

Witness (loudly): I don't know what you're driving at; how could he get it without the ticket, and that I had left with the missus?

The Court (after a pause: to an elderly barrister at counsel's table who had dined well): Mr Ryland, I wish you would take this witness in hand and see whether you can make anything of him, for I can't.

Counsel (after staring ferociously at the witness): My lord, it is my profound belief that this man is drunk.

The Court: It's a remarkable coincidence, Mr Ryland; that is precisely the idea that has been in my mind for the last ten minutes. It is disgraceful that witnesses should come into a sacred court of justice like this, in such a state of intoxication. (To the Deputy Clerk of Arraigns): Mr Mosely, don't allow this witness one farthing of expenses. I'll put a stop to this scandal if I can.[2]

Some witnesses escaped. Thus where the prisoner's father offered himself as a witness—

The Court: Let him stand down. He must know that I cannot examine him by law; he can't help knowing it. Turn him out of court.[3]

Others did not but were advised to. On an indictment for

[2] *Anon.* (n.d.) Rob. 44, P.P.
[3] *R.* v. *Hall* (1834) Arab. 15, A.P.

stealing pigs, counsel for the prisoner called Mary Hall. When she entered the box—

> *The Court:* Now, young woman, for you are a young woman, and have a child in your arms, if I catch you tripping, I will put you where the prisoner is. I have given you warning kindly: you had better say you know nothing about it.[4]

The Court was strict, however, in refusing to allow the prisoner to be questioned. Thus when a prisoner handed in a duplicate of a document, counsel asked him 'Have you any one here to prove it?'

> *The Court:* It is most irregular, ever to put any question to a prisoner.[5]

And so on an indictment for stealing sacks—

> *The prisoner:* The sacks had been in my room some time.
>
> *The Court:* Do you mean to say they were your sacks?
>
> *Doane, for prisoner:* Why, my lord, you are examining the prisoner.
>
> *The Court:* No, I am only asking him a question.
>
> *Doane:* Then, my lord, I object.
>
> *The Court:* Then you object to what you cannot comprehend.[6]

Some of the Court's rules of evidence seem to have fluctuated *de die in diem*, perhaps on principle. For—

> *The Court:* What passes at the moment, is the best evidence of what the mind feels at the instant.[7]

---

[4] *R. v. Southam* (1832) Arab. 9, P.P.

[5] *R. v. John and Jemima Davis* (1834) Arab. 15, A.P.

[6] *R. v. Murphy* (1834) Arab. 15, P.P.; and see *post.* p. 23.

[7] *R. v. Tredaway and Larkins* (1832) Arab. 8, P.P.

Thus one may consider the law applied to statements made in the absence of the accused.

> *The Court*, to witness: You must remember, and if you don't remember, you ought to know, that nothing whatever, that is said in a prisoner's absence against him, can be used in evidence under any circumstance whatever, if he was not present when it was said; and if he was, any man might be convicted and hanged in five minutes.[8]

Yet when the Court asked a witness what directions he had received, and V. Lee for the prisoner objected that such directions were given in the prisoner's absence—

> *The Court:* It is a perfectly good question, and I overrule the objection.

> *V. Lee:* It has been ruled over and over again, that such evidence is not admissible.

> *The Court:* I don't care how often it has been ruled, or who ruled it; and it was ruled against law, if it was ruled so; but I will withdraw the question.[9]

There were exceptions, too.

> *The Court:* What passes in the presence of one prisoner is evidence against the other prisoner, if they are both in the same indictment.[10]

So also when a policeman was about to state a conversation between himself and his comrade, while in pursuit, and counsel for the prisoners objected that they were out of hearing—

> *The Court:* It does not signify a button. Counsel

[8] *R.* v. *Worteldine* (1834) Arab. 6, P.P.
[9] *R.* v. *Allen* (1832) Arab. 5, A.P.
[10] *R.* v. *Prideaux and Lloyd* (1834) Arab. 6, A.P.

repeatedly make this mistake. What he said to his comrade, was not hearsay; it was about the robbery and part of the *res gesta*.[11]

The weight attached to Irish evidence was obscure. One Irish witness admitted that he had told some lies about the case, but insisted that all that he had sworn to was true.

> *The Court*, in charge: The witness is an Irishman, and people from that country, very generally, do not speak the truth when they are not on oath; but they may be believed when they are.[12]

Yet—

> *The Court*, in charge: These Irish witnesses are a good-humoured set of people, and don't much mind what they swear.
>
> *Phillips, amicus curiae:* Why, my lord, your father was an Irishman.
>
> *The Court:* I know; I only mean that they have a very pleasant roundabout way of expressing themselves; they are all eloquent.[13]

It is not easy to discern the Court's views of women. Thus—

> *The Court:* One woman is worth twenty men for a witness any day.[14]

And when a witness, who was a shoemaker, did not speak out, and said he had a cold—

> *The Court:* A man with a cold, is not fit to try a lady's shoes on.[15]

[11] *R*. v. *Gough and others* (1830) Arab. 5, A.P.
[12] *R*. v. *Heard* (1832) Arab. 8, A.P.
[13] *R*. v. *Anon.* (1832) Arab. 8, *ex rel.* C.P.
[14] *R*. v. *Collinson* (1834) Arab. 7, P.P.
[15] *R*. v. *Collinge* (1834) Arab. 7, P.P.

But to a convicted woman—

> *The Court*, to prisoner: You must go out of the country; you have disgraced even your sex.[16]

And to a female witness who did not speak out—

> *The Court*, to witness: You come here with your heads in false wigs. If you can't speak out, I'll take off your bonnet; if that won't do, you shall take your cap off; and if you don't speak out then, I'll take your hair off.[17]

And—

> *The Court*, to a female witness: If you don't speak out, I'll take off your bonnet; and you'll never get a husband.[18]

Stature counted, too.

> *The Court*, to witness: Woman, how can you be so stupid? You are tall enough, to be wise enough.[19]

Unfortunate women were in a special category.

> *The Court*, in charge: The prosecutrix in this case is an unfortunate woman. At least, she says she is an unfortunate woman, and we all know what an unfortunate woman is; at least, I know; so do you, I think; so does everybody in court; for an unfortunate woman is one who, &c.[20]

The practice of the Court and the difference between English and foreign jurisdictions was important here. Thus on an indictment for stealing a purse from the person of a professional lady—

> *The Court*, in charge: The prisoner, you see, met the

[16] *R*. v. *Mary Ann Kelly* (1833) Arab. 7.
[17] *R*. v. *Jelly* (1832) Arab. 7, A.P. *Et puis?*
[18] *R*. v. *Catherine Cox* (1834) Arab. 7, A.P.
[19] *R*. v. *Power* (1834) Arab. 7, P.P.
[20] *R*. v. *Hardy* (1838) Arab. 6, P.P., *ex rel.* D.D.K.

prosecutrix with her friend, as they were pursuing their unfortunate occupation. He joined her friend, and she walked on. Now, we collect from the practice of this Court, that this is the usual way; a man joins two girls and then one walks on. We learn from the cases here how this thing is done.[1]

And—

The Court, in charge: The witness is one of that unfortunate race, but is sworn to speak the truth, and is examined in open court, and not taken into a corner, as in foreign countries. Can you believe that the prisoner's story is grounded without foundation, and fabricated in falsehood?[2]

The Court had a strong sense of criminal geography, and of brickmaking.

The Court: I know High Wycombe; it is the worst neighbourhood on the face of the earth. The whole country is covered with brickmakers. They come from all parts of the world. I know all about them.[3]

Again,

The Court: These prisoners come here from Enfield and Edmonton, and are convicted on the clearest evidence, and the neighbourhood is very bad. I must stop it.[4]

And—

The Court, to constable: Is Barnet a very honest place?
Constable: No, my lord.

---

[1] *R.* v. *George Clark* (1833) Arab. 6, A.P.
[2] *R.* v. *Clarke* (1832) Arab. 7.
[3] *R.* v. *Rowe* (1832) Arab. 9, A.P.
[4] *R.* v. *Sheppard* (1832) Arab. 10, A.P.

The Court: No. To my certain knowledge there ought to be fifty constables there.[5]

Some localities seem to have been conclusive.

The Court, in charge: This is a case from Uxbridge. I won't say a word, as can any one doubt the prisoner's guilt?[6]

The inhabitants of Uxbridge not only were criminal but also attained the ultimate in dexterity:

The Court: I assure you, gentlemen, they will steal the very teeth out of your mouth as you walk through the streets. I know it from experience.[7]

But the rule had its exception, even though only by inadvertence:

The Court, in charge: He was a brickmaker. Now, we all know what a brickmaker's character is; at least, I do. Gentlemen, I know the prosecutor, Mr Austin, well, and there is not a kinder-hearted man in the whole county of Essex [*the prosecutor lived at Uxbridge*], and I am quite sure he can have none but a proper feeling in this case.[8]

Yet purity might harbour vice:

Per curiam: Thieves are more likely to live in the best neighbourhoods than in the worst.[9]

Some propositions were self-evident.

The Court, to policeman: Tell us all you know about this.

---

[5] *R.* v. *Cox and Turner* (1832) Arab. 9.

[6] *R.* v. *Brown* (1832) Arab. 9.

[7] *Anon., Serjeant Ballantine's Experiences* (8th ed. 1883) p. 55.

[8] *R.* v. *Southam* (1832) Arab. 9, P.P. Happily, the verdict was Not Guilty.

[9] *R.* v. *Charrington* (1831) Arab. 9, P.P.

Witness: On the day in question, I was walking along Hoxton New Town, on duty—

The Court: What's the use of telling us what everybody knows?[10]

And when Barry, for the prisoner, asked how far a new shop in Long Lane was from the old shop in Long Lane—

The Court: Come, Mr Barry, don't keep us running up and down Long Lane and Barbican. Everybody knows Long Lane: it's matter of notoriety.[11]

After all—

Per curiam: No man is fit to be a cheesemonger who cannot guess the length of a street.[12]

Some cases, too, were obvious.

The Court, in charge: I know all about these things: the pigs were fat, if they were worth £4 each. And so a man drove the cart, and another went behind to keep the pigs between him and the cart; and you see, gentlemen, that it is a great happiness in our courts, that we can see the witnesses examined, and know exactly whether they tell the truth or not. And this witness said, 'I know the coat, and I am sure of it, for it was blue or black', and he cannot be mistaken. The constable is a shrewd man, as most men in the country are, who know the habits of horses,[13] and he lets the horse go, and he finds his way to a row of houses. It was not necessary that he should go to the very house:

---

[10] *R.* v. *Knight* (1832) Arab. 8, A.P.

[11] *R.* v. *Heard* (1832) Arab. 8, A.P.

[12] *R.* v. *Robert Newby* (1833) Arab. 13, A.P.

[13] See also *post,* p. 20.

he goes to one, which is enough to satisfy the justice of the case, and nothing can be clearer.[14]

And there is the apotheosis of clarity, perhaps the most famous Arabinaic of all—

> *The Court*, in charge: If ever there was a case of clearer evidence than this of persons acting together, this case is that case.[15]

Today, some of the cases seem a little mysterious. On an indictment for burglary and stealing two ten-pound notes—

> *The Court:* Mr Barry, this case can be carried no farther: will you be so good as to jump over the moon? (*The case proceeded.*)
>
> *The Court*, in charge: Gentlemen, the only point for your consideration, is, whether the prisoner broke— that is, opened the door, or whether he only stole the notes in the dwelling-house.
>
> Verdict, Not Guilty.[16]

And when a prisoner stated that a policeman had refused to accompany him to the place where his employer was, the policeman was about to explain.

> *The Court:* Oh! you need not apologize. The police are not so polite as the Marquis of Hastings.[17]

Manifestations of guilt were diverse.

> *The Court*, in charge: I cannot suggest a doubt: she goes into a shop, and looks at several things, and purchases nothing; that always indicates some guilt.[18]

And—

[14] *R.* v. *Edwards* (1834) Arab. 14, A.P.
[15] *R.* v. *Chilston and Chandler* (1832) Arab. 9, A.P.
[16] *R.* v. *Brown, alias Peter* (1832) Arab. 6, P.P.
[17] *R.* v. *Charles Cartwright* (1833) Arab. 11, A.P.
[18] *R.* v. *Mary Santer* (1832) Arab. 7, P.P.

The Court, in charge: It is a principle in our courts, that has become an axiom, and is seldom known to have an exception, that they that hide can find; and in this case it is more than usually applicable; for, you see, the prisoner was stopped going in the very direction of the place where the property was.[19]

There were other axioms, too.

The Court, in charge: It cannot be shown that Porrett stole the goods; and then, as to Hanchett, you must acquit him. It is an axiom, a proposition.[20]

Common sense and horses each played their part.

The Court, in charge: Law is founded on common sense, and those who take it for their guide in matters of fact and plain sense, will generally come to an ultimate conclusion; and all property depends upon particular circumstances. If this had not been marked, there would not have been a mark upon it.[1]

And—

The Court, to witness: Come, sir, you are a sharp fellow. You live with horses.

Phillips, for prisoner: That don't follow.

The Court: Yes, and he is an acquaintance of the prisoner.

Phillips: But I deny the consequence, that a man becomes sharp by associating with horses.

The Court: I must discharge my duty to the public, and shall tell the jury——[2]

[19] *R.* v. *George Tolly* (1835) Arab. 8, P.P.

[20] *R.* v. *Porrett and Hanchett* (1832) Arab. 8, P.P.

[1] *R.* v. *Mahony* (1834) Arab. 14, P.P.

[2] *R.* v. *Chapman* (1831) Arab. 14, P.P. The report, alas, reveals none of the telling. See also *ante*, p. 18.

Clarity and lucidity join in:

> *The Court*, in charge: If this is a concerted story, *cadit quaestio*, as I often say; but the witness makes no bones of it, and swears positively to him; for there is a clerk with a crutch in his master's employ. He is quite clear, and he is a great fool; for he left his cart, and he swears positively to him, and he does not come here to commit perjury. Have you any doubt about it? None! Now, what honest man could have any object in turning a horse's head round the corner of a street? I have no opinion on the subject. The case is with you, and I shall only say, that the law will not allow that to be done fraudulently which it does not sanction with violence.[3]

This last thought was, perhaps, a revised version of a proposition uttered a few weeks earlier on an indictment for stealing a truck:

> *The Court*, in charge: A man shall not do by artifice and sleight of hand, that which the law does not authorise by force and violence. The facts are in a nut-shell. The broker, when you look at him, does not give a false and fabricated statement. How came the prisoner at the broker's, if he was an honest man? He takes it to the broker's: that's common sense, which guides us all. When I saw the broker get up into the box, I acted as a man in my station ought always to act, and the broker retrieved his character. Can you feel any doubt?[4]

There was human nature, too.

[3] *R.* v. *Macarthy* (1834) Arab. 13, P.P.
[4] *R.* v. *Guest and Penfold* (1834) Arab. 13, P.P.

> *The Court*, in charge: It don't take a man long to change his breeches in London.[5] Now, the witness says, she had seen the prisoner somewhere, but don't know where. That's what we all do, because she had been in the habit of seeing him every day—that is, repeatedly—at the House of Lords, holding horses, and that is human nature.[6]

Nor was the aid of the indictment to be shunned.

> *The Court*, in charge: Gentlemen, in this case it is clear that the property belonged to the rightful owner—I mean, Messrs Petrie, for their names are on the indictment. He goes into the place at once and takes away a chest, and the law presumes that it is for him to give a reasonable account of it, and that they were taken feloniously unless he can prove the contrary.[7]

The functions of the jury might be negligible or all-embracing. Thus when the prisoner said 'I was not nigh the gentlemen'—

> *The Court:* The question for the jury, is, not whether you were near him or not, for you were close to him; nor whether you took it or not, for you had it.[8]

But when counsel for the prisoner asked a witness 'Did the prosecutor state that the prisoner had been in the room where the spectacles were?'—

> *The Court:* That's matter of law, and for the jury.[9]

The effect of evidence of good character was uncertain. Sometimes it mitigated.

[5] '*Semble e contra* in the country' (Arab. 12).

[6] *R.* v. *Scott* (1832) Arab. 12, P.P.

[7] *R.* v. *John Lane* (1834) Arab. 15, P.P.

[8] *R.* v. *John Williams* (1835) Arab. 6, P.P.

[9] *R.* v. *Bloomfield* (1835) Arab. 6, A.P.

> *The Court*, in charge: The case is proved, but the prisoner has received an excellent character. He has been seven weeks in gaol, and I think you may lean to the side of mercy, and acquit him.[10]

Sometimes it aggravated. On an indictment for stealing sacks which the prisoner said had been in his room for some time, a coat being with the sacks—

> *The Court*, in charge: His character is good, but that makes no difference: if he had a good character, that makes it so much the worse; for he had a good master. He said, it was his till the true owner was found; that makes it ten times the worse. He says, it was wearing apparel; that makes it ten times worse in addition.[11]

Again, in one case a prisoner was convicted on one indictment and the prosecution declined to proceed on a second indictment. One of the witnesses, butler to the prosecutrix, then stated that the prisoner had behaved well, and had borne the highest character for five years while in his employ.

> *The Court:* Do you wish the prisoner to be tried on a second indictment, and transported for fourteen years? because, if you do, go on in that way.[12]

And where counsel for the prisoner observed that only one witness had been called, though three were present—

> *The Court:* Now, don't make me transport him for life.[13]

Where evidence of good character was given by a Jew—

[10] *R.* v. *Cashman* (1832) Arab. 12, P.P., *ex rel.* R.N.C.
[11] *R.* v. *Murphy* (1834) Arab. 15, P.P.; and see *ante*, p. 12.
[12] *R.* v. *Tate* (1832) Arab. 10, A.P.
[13] *R.* v. *Clark* (1832) Arab. 10, P.P. But here the verdict was Not Guilty.

The Court, in charge: Now, gentlemen, you have heard the case; and the Jew says, that the prisoner has borne a good character; and that he, the Jew, never heard anything against him. All I shall say to that, is, *Credat Judaeus Apollo*. If he does, I don't, and dare say you won't, gentlemen.[14]

Recommendations to mercy also produced diverse responses. Where the jury convicted the accused of larceny, but recommended him to mercy, believing him to have been in distress, the reaction was unremarkable.

The Court, to prisoner: Let me not see you here again. If you are in distress, you must apply to the proper authorities, and not take the law into your own hands and steal.[15]

Yet when a prisoner was convicted and the prosecutor recommended him to mercy, believing him to have been the dupe of others—

The Court: Oh! that makes it so much the worse.[16]

As for pleas *ad misericordiam*, when a prisoner said that he had a wife and four children—

The Court: Never mind. You may have twenty wives and twenty children, but you must not abuse the public.[17]

None the less, the powers of the Court remained extensive.

The Court: Prisoner at the Bar, you have been found guilty on several indictments, and it is in my power to

---

[14] *R.* v. *Anon.* (n.d.) Arab. 5, *ex rel.* J.H. *et al.* Horace's words were 'Credat Judaeus Apella' ('Let the Jew Apella believe that', or, more freely, 'Tell that to the marines'): *Satires*, I, v, 100.

[15] *R.* v. *Charles Levens* (1833) Arab. 11, A.P.

[16] *R.* v. *Robert Edwards* (1833) Arab. 11, A.P.

[17] *R.* v. *Faulkner* (1834) Arab. 15, A.P., *ex rel.* F.P.W.

subject you to transportation for a period very considerably beyond the term of your natural life; but the Court, in its mercy, will not go as far as it lawfully might go, and the sentence is that you be transported for two periods of seven years each.[18]

Again—

> *The Court:* Prisoner at the Bar, there are mitigating circumstances in this case that induce me to take a lenient view of it; and I will therefore give you a chance of redeeming a character that you have irretrievably lost.[19]

How can a book even so short as this be summed up? Only the Court could do this; and it did. Two dicta suffice.

> *Prisoner:* I want to ask, whether it is likely—
>
> *The Court:* We have nothing to do with what is likely or unlikely: so many unlikely things happen in courts of justice, that the public time must not be wasted on such inquiries.[20]

And—

> *The Court:* I'll be bound there is not such a Court in the universe as this—not in the kingdom, and the whole British empire.[21]

Curia ipsa dixit.

[18] *Anon.* (n.d.) Rob. 43.   [20] *R.* v. *Thomas Brown* (1835) Arab. 16, P.P.
[19] *Anon.* (n.d.) Rob. 48.   [21] *R.* v. *Pope* (1834) Arab. 11, P.P.

Index